Real Solutions *for* Busy Moms

DEVOTIONAL

52 GOD-INSPIRED
MESSAGES *for* YOUR HEART

Real
Solutions
for
Busy
Moms

DEVOTIONAL

Kathy Ireland

HOWARD BOOKS
A DIVISION OF SIMON & SCHUSTER, INC.
New York Nashville London Toronto Sydney

Published by Howard Books, a division of Simon & Schuster, Inc.
1230 Avenue of the Americas, New York, NY 10020
www.howardpublishing.com

Real Solutions for Busy Moms Devotional © 2009 by Kathy Ireland Worldwide, LLC

ISBN 978-1-4165-6352-5
ISBN 978-1-4391-6696-3 (ebook)

10 9 8 7 6 5 4 3 2 1

Manufactured in the United States of America

For information regarding special discounts for bulk purchases, please contact: Simon & Schuster Special Sales at 1-866-506-1949 or business@simonandschuster.com.

The Simon & Schuster Speakers Bureau can bring authors to your live event. For more information or to book an event, contact the Simon & Schuster Speakers Bureau at 1-866-248-3049 or visit our website at www.simonspeakers.com.

Edited by Chrys Howard
Cover design by LeftCoast Designs
Interior design by Jaime Putorti

*This book is dedicated to the love of my life,
whom I love more with each passing year, my
amazing husband, Greg, and the lights of our lives,
our precious children, Erik, Lily, and Chloe, who
bring us an overflowing wealth of joy.*

contents

introduction

*U*nless we live in isolation, we are all so busy. "So much to do, so little time" is no longer a cliché. It is reality. The tech age we're living in doesn't always allow us the energy to live the life of our dreams. Are you too busy with chores, work, and responsibilities and fear to let God direct you? Are you following His plan for your life?

I became a Christian at the age of eighteen. I was alone and in a foreign country where I felt insecure and unsafe. I reached into my suitcase out of boredom and found a Bible my mother had packed for me. It opened to the Gospel of Matthew, and my life changed forever. When I read His Word, I knew the pure bliss of God's truth. My heart was filled. I had always believed in God, but that was the start of the most incredible and in fact only perfect relationship I have ever known or will experience in this life.

God's love for us is the only real solution that we can depend upon. Jesus Christ is my best friend, Savior, and Lord. He is the Rock upon whom I build my life. Everything that happens in my life that is good is a gift from Him. I have too often moved away from Him. Not found time for Him. Not sought His infinite wisdom and counsel. Thankfully, He never moves away from me . . . despite my arrogance and disobedience. Please learn from my sins and misdeeds. God is beside you. Please do not harden your heart to His call. Sadly, I remained a baby Christian for far too long. Where I was an infant, I pray I am learning to toddle.

Now I understand that I need to open my Bible and read each day. Being too tired for God does not work for me. Life is better when each day starts with Him. I keep signs in our home that celebrate J.O.Y.! reminding me that **J**esus, **O**thers, and **Y**ou is a wonderful way to live.

Everyone faces problems, and if this devotional can become a start for your daily conversations with our Lord, I will be humbled beyond words. This is the sixth book I've written, and I am so blessed to be able to share these solutions and messages, which are God-inspired with your heart.

You may wonder if, as my heart speaks to you, I can relate to the crisis you're facing today. Please know, my life is filled with amazing joys and unsurprising valleys: illness, tears, financial problems, weight issues, hurting people you love, being hurt by people you love, the unexpected death of a loved one, having a miscarriage on the same day we learned we were pregnant, being told—incorrectly—that one of our children would be born with special needs, seeing my husband fight his way back to life from a coma in a near-fatal accident and almost drowning in the ocean myself, seeing fellow Christians fight each other rather than working together to help others, drug and alcohol issues, squabbles and fights that didn't have to happen. I've encountered everything here and am still praying and growing as a Christian in dealing with it all. Having a long-ago modeling career in the last century and making a living in design, thankfully doesn't keep me from facing the turbulence that we call life.

Some people wish that I wasn't so direct and outspoken. My job was once to "shut up and pose!" I guess I'm making up for the years I sat in silence. Scripture promises that God will restore the years eaten away by the locusts. I've decided not to waste anyone's time by worrying about whether or not people agree with me, as I once did. Fence-sitting is boring and dishonest. We can disagree. That's all right! Let's just do it in faith, honor, and His love, which commands respect for each person He made.

One example of a stance that some people want me to be silent about is the precious gift of life. My position on the unborn is controversial and some say conservative. I believe that saving life at every stage is liberal. It is protection. The unborn need our support. If we do not stand for them on this earth, who will?

While fighting for life, I will also never judge a woman who has had an abortion. One of my greatest fears, is that in judging and condemning anyone, I may keep them from knowing our Lord and that is something that concerns me very deeply.

Please review this book each week. And keep your Bible nearby. The Bible is the best book ever written for life management. It has a solution for every problem that you will ever face.

If this middle-aged mother of three, wife, and working mom (by the way—all moms work whether they get paid or not) can offer words of comfort and experience that lead you toward your closer walk with Him, then . . . mission accomplished!

Please know that although we've never met, I feel we are starting a friendship. We are related in Christ, and you reached out to me today when you opened your heart to this book.

Thank you and God bless you!
Love, Kathy

Real Solutions
for Busy Moms

DEVOTIONAL

1

make money your servant

Each month, we are falling deeper into debt. We're spending money we don't have, and now I'm worried about keeping my job. To be honest, I'm scared!

THE LORD'S SOLUTION

Blessed is the man who finds wisdom and the man who gains understanding. For her profit is better than the profit of silver and her gain better than fine gold.

PROVERBS 3:13–14

Wealth obtained by fraud dwindles, but the one who gathers by labor increases it.

PROVERBS 13:11

MOM TO MOM

As Christians, we know that there is no such thing as "financial security." The only real security in this life and the next comes from being one with the Lord. The current financial crisis is impacting everyone. No one knows what tomorrow holds, but as believers, we know who holds tomorrow. Most people believe that more money will solve their financial problems. But if your tendency is to spend every dollar that comes in, for whatever reason, more money will never solve anything. You and your family will always be struggling with debt and living from one paycheck to the next. Early in my modeling career, I began spending most of my income and paying less attention to saving. Then I blew out my knee while skiing, and suddenly the dollars stopped flowing. That experience was a powerful lesson for me. It taught me the importance of living beneath my means. After that, I made sure to set aside a specific portion of my income every month. Remember, God wants us to be wise with our money. You are the mistress, and your money is your servant. If you maintain a healthy relationship with money, you'll be a great model for your children, and your family will be on its way to financial success.

ACTION STEPS

1. Read what the Bible has to say about money, such as Matthew 25:14–30, Luke 16:13, and Proverbs 15:16.

2. If you're not doing so already, establish a budget and stick

to it. Look for expenditures that could be eliminated or at least cut back while you're in debt.

3. If your financial problems are severe, consider more drastic steps such as relocating to an area where living expenses and real estate values are lower. It's hard and scary, sure, but achieving peace of mind and financial stability is worth it!

Dear God, I thank You for the financial blessings You've given us and ask for Your forgiveness for how I've managed them. Please grant me new wisdom as we take charge of our family's finances.

2

peace in our time

Today has been a disaster! Too many diapers, too many dirty dishes, too many demands. Where can I find peace of mind, because right now I feel like I'm losing my mind? How do I find hope and joy?

THE LORD'S SOLUTION

May the God of hope fill you with all joy and peace in believing, so that you will abound in hope by the power of the Holy Spirit.

ROMANS 15:13

Be still, and know that I am God.

PSALM 46:10 (NIV)

MOM TO MOM

Please understand that those hurried and harried feelings can weigh down any mom. The answer is to spend more time with the source of peace and rest. Recently, I began setting my alarm clock anywhere from fifteen minutes to an hour earlier than usual. I now dedicate those first morning minutes to studying the Bible and talking with and listening to God. Starting each day by focusing on Him is making a huge difference in my life. When I don't make time for God, my priorities get out of alignment and I have great trouble coping. When that special appointment with our Lord is honored, He gives me the strength, hope, and peace to find solutions for the challenges that continually arise. This works for me . . . it may work for you too.

ACTION STEPS

1. Find at least fifteen minutes out of your busy day to reflect on God's love for you. Read Romans 15:13 and let your heart fill up with joy and peace.

2. When the day presents a serious challenge, pause from the situation and pray, even if in silence, for guidance and wisdom, knowing that God will answer your prayer. He won't necessarily give you the answer you want, but He always answers, and His plan is always the right one.

Father, thank You for loving me so much, for always being ready to offer comfort, hope, and peace. Show me how to put distractions aside so that I can rest in You.

3

---

put on your oxygen mask first

❧

I know that I need to take care of myself—eat healthy, exercise, get more sleep—but there's never enough time. I feel like my family needs me every hour of the day! Aren't their needs more important than my own?

THE LORD'S SOLUTION

Do you not know that your body is a temple of the Holy Spirit who is in you, whom you have from God, and that you are not your own? For you have been bought with a price: therefore glorify God in your body.

1 CORINTHIANS 6:19–20

I pray that in all respects you may prosper and be in good health, just as your soul prospers.

3 JOHN 1:2

MOM TO MOM

Healthy living is a huge challenge for us busy moms. We're pulled in a thousand different directions, and usually every one of those tugs feels critically important. There was a time in my life when every minute of every day was focused around our children's needs and the responsibilities of our business. Taking time to exercise or plan healthy meals for my husband and me seemed like a luxury I couldn't afford. I barely had time to brush my teeth! It was during this period that a friend lovingly reminded me of what flight attendants tell you at the beginning of every plane trip: "Put on your own oxygen mask before you try to put on someone else's." It's true—you can't help others, including your husband, your children, or your friends, if you're incapacitated yourself. Healthy eating, regular exercise, and occasional times to recover and refresh aren't just optional; they're essential. God loves and values you, so love yourself enough to care for your needs. You'll be much better equipped to be a powerful mom for your family.

ACTION STEPS

1. If you're not a nutrition expert, get familiar with the famous food pyramid (www.pyramid.gov). Skip the crash diets and start a routine of healthy eating.

2. Choose sports or activities you enjoy—such as walking, jogging, swimming, cycling, tennis, hiking, or aerobics—and incorporate them into your lifestyle. If it's fun for you, you're much more likely to stay with it.

3. Schedule a time each week that's just for you. Don't be afraid to ask your husband, a sister, a friend, or a neighbor for help with the kids. Yes, family is a major priority, and you are a member of the family too.

Lord, I do want to honor You by taking care of the body You have given me. Please help me to balance caring for my family with caring for myself so I can be the wife and mother You've designed me to be.

4

give your kids what they need to succeed

Our children are learning about reproduction at school. I know I should ask if they have any questions, but I'm too embarrassed to bring it up. Is it all right to wait for their questions? Or do I need to take the lead?

THE LORD'S SOLUTION

I will instruct you and teach you in the way which you should go; I will counsel you with My eye upon you.

PSALM 32:8

Now then go, and I, even I, will be with your mouth, and teach you what you are to say.

EXODUS 4:12

MOM TO MOM

In your heart, you have the clarity and the wisdom to know that, as the parent, you must take the lead. Your question is dealing with embarrassment rather than reality. Our children live in a dangerous world. Pornography, premarital sex, and alcohol and drug use are just some of the snares that can entrap our sons and daughters. It often seems so overwhelming. What are we moms to do? We can start by telling our children the truth about the temptations and risks. For example, only you can decide when it's the right time to discuss sex with your kids. But please don't put off "the talk" because you feel awkward or embarrassed. Would you rather they hear the facts from you or from someone else who may not share your values? Get over your embarrassment, and make it a priority to discuss these important issues. Don't stop after one conversation—establish a continuing and open dialogue. The Lord has assigned us moms to prepare our children to go into the world, and part of our job is to give them the essential information they'll need to succeed.

ACTION STEPS

1. Decide if it's time to talk with your children about issues such as premarital sex, pornography, and alcohol and drug use. Think beforehand about what you want to say; do research if needed!

2. Schedule a time for you and your child to have a relaxed, one-on-one conversation. When you get together, remember

to listen as well as talk. Give your children plenty of opportunities to ask questions. Make it clear that you're always willing to discuss whatever is on your child's mind. Please don't make your children feel they need an appointment to receive your undivided attention. If they have to wait and it's truly important, they may find themselves going to someone else for answers and attention. That's a potential crisis waiting to happen, and predators exploit these kinds of opportunities.

Dear Jesus, please protect our children from this world's temptations and dangers! Please give me the confidence and the right words to discuss all issues with my kids so they will be properly prepared for the challenges ahead.

5

Jesus, others, you

My life is no longer my own. I can't prioritize anything. What's wrong with me?

THE LORD'S SOLUTION

Consider it all joy, my brethren, when you encounter various trials.

JAMES 1:2

Rejoice in the Lord always; again I will say, rejoice!

PHILIPPIANS 4:4

MOM TO MOM

Do you know what your priorities are? If so, and if it is where you invest most of your time and passion, you're much more likely to be joyful. When I write out my priorities, my faith in Jesus Christ tops the list. He is my foundation, my daily source of purpose and joy. One of the little things I do to remind myself of this is to take a sheet of paper and write in big capital letters, *JOY*. After each letter, I fill in a word: Jesus, Others, You. I keep one of these JOY signs on my bathroom mirror and another in my kitchen. On days when I'm feeling more stressed than joyful, those signs stop me in midstep. I'll think, *Okay, wait a second . . . maybe I need to rearrange my priorities at this moment.* And when I do that, the joy returns. Whatever your priorities are, I encourage you to keep them in front of you. If you stay attuned to what matters most to you, you'll find it much easier to adopt an attitude of joy each day.

ACTION STEPS

1. Make a list of your priorities and passions. Ask yourself: *Am I actively pursuing the things that matter most to me?*

2. Decide what you can do to better align your life with your priorities and take steps to make that happen. You might start by putting up a reminder on your bathroom mirror!

Lord, I so often forget to make You first priority in my life. No wonder I'm missing out on joy! Help me to rejoice in You no matter what else is going on. Thank You for loving me!

6

---

digging out of debt

I'm a single mother and am drowning in debt. My credit cards are maxed out, and I'm worried the bank will foreclose on our home. I'm ready to give up, declare bankruptcy, and start over.

THE LORD'S SOLUTION

God is our refuge and strength, a very present help in trouble.

PSALM 46:1

We count blessed those who endured.

JAMES 5:11

MOM TO MOM

I understand how overwhelming a financial crisis can be, especially for a single mom. You feel as if you're running in quicksand—the harder you try, the farther you sink. Bankruptcy, however, is rarely a good solution. When you walk away from financial commitments, you damage more than your credit rating. Bankruptcy will destroy your financial reputation and your ability to achieve your financial goals. And what will it do to your self-confidence? When you face serious medical issues or hopeless litigation or are a victim of fraud, you may have little choice. Usually, however, there are options. I encourage you to try some of the steps listed below. Remember that God is with you and that He watches for and honors your resolve to do the right thing: "I know your deeds, and your . . . service and perseverance" (Revelation 2:19). No matter how bleak your situation, the Lord is at your side and ready to guide you to the next step if you will persevere and trust in Him.

ACTION STEPS

1. Call your credit-card company and your bank and ask them to lower your interest rate. Lenders don't want you to sink so low that they lose you as a customer.

2. Explore ways to bring in extra funds. Can you host a yard sale? Sell a few items on eBay? Babysit for your neighbors?

3. Consider asking for a raise at work. Talk about the value of your performance, not that you really need the money.

4. Do all you can to pay more than your minimum monthly payment.

5. If credit cards are too tempting, cut them up and convert to a cash system.

6. Seek advice from a professional financial adviser, a non-profit credit counseling service, or a friend who's wise with money.

Lord Jesus, I know that Your wisdom, power, and love are bigger than my financial crisis. I do want to persevere and trust wholeheartedly in You. Please give me the guidance I need to resolve my money problems.

7

joy will return

Four years ago, our infant son passed away. People say that time heals all wounds. I'm still angry and still in shock. I've never felt this kind of grief, pain, and rage before. Why did God allow this to happen? How do I get through this?

THE LORD'S SOLUTION

*You will have the L*ORD *for an everlasting light, and the days of your mourning will be over.*

ISAIAH 60:20

We also exult in our tribulations, knowing that tribulation brings about perseverance; and perseverance, proven character; and proven character, hope; and hope does not disappoint, because the love of God has been poured out within our hearts through the Holy Spirit.

ROMANS 5:3–5

MOM TO MOM

It is impossible for me to fully comprehend why unspeakable tragedies happen every day. We ask ourselves, *Why does God intervene in one circumstance and apparently not intervene in another?* I don't pretend to have all the answers, but I can tell you this: God is true to His every Word. He will bring comfort in every situation when we embrace Him: "For just as the sufferings of Christ are ours in abundance, so also our comfort is abundant through Christ" (2 Corinthians 1:5). Sadness is an important package we must give to our Lord. This does not mean we are free from pain. Far from it! We feel the pain, but we focus on our faith and move forward by living in God's promises. Know that renewal is coming. Hang on to the knowledge that just as spring follows winter, joy will return to your life, no matter how painful the journey.

ACTION STEPS

1. God bless you and your family. There is no specific timetable for coping with a great loss . Please consult your pastor, pray with friends and family, and seek professional help to begin the long healing process. I cannot imagine a greater loss in this life. Years ago, Greg and I experienced a miscarriage on the same day we learned we were expecting a baby. The loss of that life is still very real to us. Please take your grief to the Lord in prayer. He understands your pain, your confusion, your anger, and your tears like no one else. Allow Him to bathe you in comfort and peace.

2. Reach out to someone, even if it's just with a smile or hug. Compassion leads to joy for the giver as well as the receiver.

Dear God, I don't understand why You allow so much sorrow and pain in our lives, yet I know that You love us and want the best for us. I need You now more than ever—please grant me the courage to keep going and to keep on placing my trust in You.

8

---

push through the fear

I seem to be a fearful person. I'm afraid to address certain subjects with my husband and kids, and I'm afraid to talk to my friends about my faith. Why?

THE LORD'S SOLUTION

*Trust in the L*ORD *with all your heart and do not lean on your own understanding.*

PROVERBS 3:5

In God I have put my trust, I shall not be afraid. What can man do to me?

PSALM 56:11

MOM TO MOM

Rejection is often painful. We who believe in and are fortunate enough to love Jesus must stand our ground and speak His Word. We don't have to preach. We just have to be honest about our relationship with Him. In public, that can make us nervous. Most surveys indicate that public speaking is the single greatest fear for men and women (death is second!). I can relate to that. I remember being so nervous before my first business speech that I wanted to crawl under the table. A friend sitting next to me offered some wise advice: "Kathy, you need to get over yourself," he said. "This isn't about you. There are people out there who need your best, who need the information and insights you have to offer. You're in a unique position to share what they want to hear. So go for it!" He was right. Each of us has gifts and knowledge we need to pass on, whether it's with our families or the world. When we don't, we fall short of our purpose and rob someone else of our best. I believe our fear usually stems from a lack of trust in ourselves and the plan God has laid out for us. Learn to feel the fear and move forward anyway. You'll be helping others as you move closer to God's destiny for your life.

ACTION STEPS

1. Set aside an hour to read God's Word on the topic of fear, such as 2 Timothy 1:7, Romans 8:15–16, 1 John 4:18, Psalm 91:1–2, and Psalm 23:4–5. Pray specifically about whatever you are afraid of, and ask the Lord to calm your heart.

2. Practice feeling the fear and pushing through it. Start with small steps, and give God the freedom to lead the way.

Heavenly Father, please forgive me for my lack of trust and faith in You. I know that Your love and power are greater than any obstacle I will face. Help me to set aside my fears and rely more each day upon You.

9

the joy of giving

I feel guilty because we rarely give money away, even though there are so many good causes. It's a battle just to balance our budget each week. At our income level, I doubt our contributions make much difference anyway.

THE LORD'S SOLUTION

Remember the LORD your God, for it is He who is giving you power to make wealth.

DEUTERONOMY 8:18

You shall surely tithe all the produce from what you sow, which comes out of the field every year.

DEUTERONOMY 14:22

MOM TO MOM

I can't speak for others, but because of my faith, the practice of tithing—giving 10 percent of all we earn back to God—is very important to me. I believe that everything, including my money, belongs to God. He can make good use of even the smallest gift. For example, just five dollars will buy netting to protect an entire family in Africa from mosquitoes that spread malaria. And if you're familiar with the story of the poor widow (Luke 21:1–4) who gave two small coins—all that she had—you know that Jesus honors those who give beyond what they can easily afford. In addition to encouraging those in need, our giving opens the door for God to bless us: "'Test Me now in this,' says the LORD of hosts, 'if I will not open for you the windows of heaven and pour out for you a blessing until it overflows'" (Malachi 3:10). One of the greatest of those blessings is the joy we discover from helping others.

ACTION STEPS

1. Read 2 Corinthians 8:1–15. Spend time in prayer, asking God what this might mean for your life.

2. Take another look at your budget. Consider how you might be able to change your spending habits so you don't miss out on the joy of giving.

Lord, I am reminded today that everything I have is truly Yours. Thank You for so many blessings, which I often take for granted. Show me how You would have me use those blessings to reach out to others.

10

quick to hear

I have a problem with my temper. So often, when my kids say or do something I don't approve of, I go into "attack mode" and say things I later regret.

THE LORD'S SOLUTION

When there are many words, transgression is unavoidable, but he who restrains his lips is wise.

PROVERBS 10:19

The mouth of the righteous utters wisdom, and his tongue speaks justice.

PSALM 37:30

MOM TO MOM

The tongue is a powerful instrument. It can be used to praise, encourage, and inform, or it can be a weapon that destroys. I urge you, whenever you're interacting with family and friends—*especially* if you feel your temperature rising—to remember these words from Scripture: "Everyone must be quick to hear, slow to speak and slow to anger" (James 1:19). God doesn't make mistakes. He gave us two ears and one mouth because we need to be listening twice as much as we're talking. The only exception is when we're listening to hurtful words. Gossip, for example, can do terrible harm to reputations and relationships. If you find yourself talking with someone who is spreading rumors, try this: stop the gossiper midstory and say, "Let me go and get the person you're talking about so we can have a constructive conversation." When we use our ears and tongues wisely, we build up rather than tear down those around us—and we please the Lord at the same time.

ACTION STEPS

1. The next time you are tempted to respond to your kids with an angry retort, stop before you speak. Try to see the situation from their point of view. It's often more important to keep the communication channels open than to convert your children to your point of view.

2. Think about your gatherings with friends. Does gossip ever creep into your conversations? If so, decide what you

can do to steer the talk in a new direction—or cut off the gossip before it starts.

Lord Jesus, I admit that I am not always quick to listen and slow to speak. I want to communicate in ways that are uplifting to others and honoring to You. Please give me the strength and wisdom to be the example I need to be for my family and all those in my life.

11

listen to your voice

Between my family, my part-time job, and volunteering, I never have a minute to myself. At the end of most days, I realize I haven't even sat down! I feel like I'm close to a breakdown.

THE LORD'S SOLUTION

The God of all grace . . . will Himself perfect, confirm, strengthen and establish you.

1 PETER 5:10

He makes me lie down in green pastures; He leads me beside quiet waters. He restores my soul.

PSALM 23:2–3

MOM TO MOM

A movie critic once wrote that I had a voice that could kill small animals. I was hurt by this comment, but it did make me listen more closely to my speaking voice. It may be time for you to listen to your voice too—the one inside that is too often drowned out by others' priorities. What whispers from the deepest part of your soul have you ignored? What needs have you neglected? When we stuff down our feelings, they usually reappear in unhealthy forms such as anger, overeating, or depression. Find some quiet time and listen to what your mind and body are telling you. I'll bet you hear that you need to be a better friend to yourself. Do you know what refreshes and energizes you? Is it exercise? Music? Time alone? A night at the movies? When was the last time you did any of those things? Allow the Lord to guide you toward more of these encouraging activities so that you, too, can say, "He leads me beside quiet waters. He restores my soul."

ACTION STEPS

1. List ten things that bring joy and renewed strength into your life. Beside each item on your list, write out a brief plan that details how you can incorporate that wonderful energy-builder into your lifestyle. If you can't afford it, develop a saving plan so that eventually it will become a reality.

2. Begin taking care of your needs *today*. If you must start small, set aside at least fifteen minutes for yourself every

morning and afternoon or evening. Protect that time as if you're meeting with a long-lost friend—because you are.

Dear God, You know that I struggle with managing my time and taking care of myself. I need Your help to be restored and reenergized. Show me the way, Lord, as I seek to be a better friend to myself.

12

do I really need church?

I believe in God and read the Bible. With everything else happening in my family's life, church seems like one more obligation. Is it really that important?

THE LORD'S SOLUTION

Now you are Christ's body, and individually members of it.

1 CORINTHIANS 12:27

Let us consider how to stimulate one another to love and good deeds, not forsaking our own assembling together, as is the habit of some, but encouraging one another.

HEBREWS 10:24–25

MOM TO MOM

Early in my faith life, stubbornness and disobedience limited my spiritual growth. During those years I didn't believe it was necessary to belong to a church. I read the Bible, I believed in God, I had a relationship with the Lord. Why commit time I didn't really have to hang out with people I didn't know? I realize now how important finding a "home" church truly is for strength and growth. When we worship and spend time with people who are on the same spiritual journey, we discover new resources for support, understanding, and accountability. We come together and lean on each other. We ask questions and find answers to the problems that can't be resolved on our own. Each of us has something to give to the body of Christ. And we can receive even more.

ACTION STEPS

1. When choosing a church, ask if the Bible is viewed as the Word of God and if the focus is on reading the Bible. You'll want more than stories and entertainment.

2. Check out your prospective church's youth programs. Will this be a place your children get excited about? Does it have leaders and mentors who will play positive roles in your children's lives? Are there opportunities for kids to get together on more than Sunday mornings?

3. Ask if your prospective church has an open-book policy on its budget. Good stewardship is one sign of a church that's on the right path.

4. Trust your intuition. When you walk in the doors, do you feel the presence of the Holy Spirit? Do you feel called upon to make a difference here? Pray about it, and discuss it with your family.

Father, I admit that I usually prefer to be a spiritual Lone Ranger rather than interact with other believers. Help me to break out of this thinking so our family can develop new relationships with brothers and sisters in Christ.

13

healthy rebellion

I'm worried about the new friends my fourteen-year-old is hanging out with. I suspect that some of them are into drugs. I don't think my son is, but how do I keep it that way?

THE LORD'S SOLUTION

Flee from youthful lusts and pursue righteousness, faith, love and peace, with those who call on the Lord from a pure heart.

2 TIMOTHY 2:22

In all your ways acknowledge Him, and He will make your paths straight.

PROVERBS 3:6

MOM TO MOM

Peer pressure certainly plays a major role in teenage drug use, but there are steps you can take to encourage your kids to make wise choices. It starts with talking with them about the law and physical and emotional risks associated with alcohol and drug use and abuse. Explain your own feelings and listen to theirs. Most kids want to rebel at some point in their lives. Tell them that this is their chance! I rebelled at times against the "in" crowd when I was younger. When I was at a party and someone offered me drugs, I said no. When a photographer asked me early in my modeling career to take off my top, I said I wasn't comfortable doing that. He insisted and shoved me, and unfortunately I had to shove back. I'm not a violent person, and I pray that was appropriate rebellion. It's a great comfort to remember that Jesus was a rebel too. He broke with custom by treating women with unusual kindness and respect and by teaching and healing on the Sabbath. Remind your sons and daughters that instead of trying to fit in, what's most important is being true to yourself and the plan God has for you.

ACTION STEPS

1. In addition to talking with your children, watch for signs of drug abuse such as sudden changes in appetite, energy, or personality. If you have suspicions, don't feel that you're violating your child's privacy by insisting on drug testing.

2. Take away temptation. Remove or lock away all alcohol and drugs in your home, including prescription drugs.

3. Pray daily for protection and wisdom for your children.

Dear Lord, it's scary to watch my kids grow up in this fallen world. Give me the words to guide them toward wise decisions. Surround them with angels to protect them each day from harm.

14

you are not alone

I'm a single mother with two children. We're struggling in so many ways. I feel lonely and overwhelmed. I just don't think I can do this!

THE LORD'S SOLUTION

O LORD, You have heard the desire of the humble; You will strengthen their heart, You will incline Your ear.

PSALM 10:17

The LORD your God is a compassionate God; He will not fail you nor destroy you.

DEUTERONOMY 4:31

MOM TO MOM

Motherhood is an incredible challenge for any woman, but doubly so for the single mom. It takes great skill and courage to raise a family when all the responsibilities that go with parenting and putting food on the table, as well as every other large and small decision, rest on your shoulders. Single parent or not, you need a support system. Family and friends are potential resources. So are your church and wonderful programs such as the Boys & Girls Clubs of America. The best resource to turn to, however, is always Jesus. He will be there for you no matter how bleak your circumstances: "Come to Me, all who are weary and heavy-laden, and I will give you rest" (Matthew 11:28). No problem is too big for Him to handle. No dilemma is new to Him. Know that when you reach out to Jesus in praise and prayer, He will respond. You are not alone. His promise is that He will be "with you always, even to the end of the age" (Matthew 28:20).

ACTION STEPS

1. Put this book down right now. Pour out your troubles to the Lord in prayer. Praise Him for the blessings He has provided in your life and for those you haven't yet received.

2. Listen and wait patiently for the Lord's answers to your requests. Sometimes we miss His solution because we are too frantic to hear it.

3. Though it may not feel like it, consider that your struggles and loneliness may actually be an opportunity to deepen

your relationship with the Lord. Allow Him to fill your soul with His presence.

Lord Jesus, I love You and need You! I get so stressed out and lonely sometimes. Please send me supportive friends who can share my burdens, and please don't ever leave my side. Thank You for giving me hope even when I feel hopeless.

15

get comfortable with being uncomfortable

My daughter has been invited to a sleepover at a friend's house. I barely know her parents and wonder about their values. I want to let my daughter go to the sleepover, but I'm not comfortable with grilling her friend's parents about their rules and standards.

THE LORD'S SOLUTION

Many are the afflictions of the righteous.

PSALM 34:19

We sent Timothy . . . to strengthen and encourage you as to your faith, so that no one would be disturbed by these afflictions; for you yourselves know that we have been destined for this.

1 THESSALONIANS 3:2–3

MOM TO MOM

As teachers and protectors of our children, we moms often confront times when we need to initiate a difficult discussion. Sometimes it's with our children themselves. Sometimes it is with the friends of our children or their parents. No one feels comfortable doing this, of course. But when the issue is our family's well-being, comfort is irrelevant. Does God promise us that we will be comfortable as we go through life? Just the opposite! According to Jesus, "In the world you have tribulation" (John 16:33). If your first priorities are anything like mine—faith and family—you know that comfort ranks far down on the list. Our desire for comfort may really be a method of denial about whatever problem is facing us or our kids. Maybe it's time to get comfortable with being uncomfortable! The ultimate discomfort, after all, is not being at one with the Lord and falling short of the responsibility He's given us as moms.

ACTION STEPS

1. Ask yourself how you're doing as a teacher and protector of your children. Are there times when you choose to stay in your comfort zone instead of confronting important issues? How can you encourage yourself to stretch out of that comfort zone? (Read Scripture passages such as Proverbs 28:1 and 2 Timothy 1:7.)

2. Schedule a time to talk with your kids about their friends and their friends' families. Ask for *their* impressions of the

values these families hold. Your willingness to start the conversation may open up a wonderful dialogue about what matters to your family and why.

Heavenly Father, help me to remember that my comfort can never compare to the safety of my children. Please give me the wisdom and courage to investigate and speak out when the well-being of my family is at stake, no matter how uncomfortable that makes me.

16

the privilege of obedience

I am a Christian, and I read my Bible often, but there are a few messages I simply don't agree with. They don't seem to fit today's world or feel right for my life. How do you handle this dilemma?

THE LORD'S SOLUTION

If anyone loves Me, he will keep My word; and My Father will love him, and We will come to him and make Our abode with him.

JOHN 14:23

This is the love of God, that we keep His commandments.

1 JOHN 5:3

MOM TO MOM

Maybe you can relate to this—I'm a pretty stubborn person. When I invited Jesus into my heart, I made a new best friend who would love me and guide the rest of my life. I remained a "baby Christian," though, for too long. Reading through the Bible, I would pick and choose what to apply to my life. Some passages were great. Others I thought either didn't pertain to me or must have contained typos. I was guilty of trying to mold the Lord into what I wanted Him to be rather than allowing Him to mold me into the person I was born to be. Though I still have a great distance to travel in my spiritual journey, I realize today that it is so important to accept and be obedient to His Word. When we set aside our agendas and follow His direction, we experience the full pleasure and blessing of being in His will. Jesus said, "If you love Me, you will keep My commandments" (John 14:15). Obedience to the Lord is much more than a responsibility or obligation—it is a privilege that expresses our heartfelt love to Him.

ACTION STEPS

1. Spend a few minutes reflecting on this Scripture passage: "Obey My voice, and I will be your God, and you will be My people; and you will walk in all the way which I command you, that it may be well with you" (Jeremiah 7:23). Ask yourself why obedience is so important to God—and why it's important to you as a parent.

2. List areas where obedience is a struggle for you. Pray about them. Ask Jesus to clear your mind and unbind your heart so you can love Him through obedience.

Dear Jesus, I must often seem like a wayward child to You. Help me to see that my own self-centered ideas and desires can never compare with Your eternal wisdom. Show me the path to obedience in all my thoughts and actions.

17

managing messages

My son is five years old; my daughter is three. I'm afraid that the crazy images and messages rampant in the media today will warp them as they grow up. How do I protect them from all that?

THE LORD'S SOLUTION

I will set no worthless thing before my eyes; . . . it shall not fasten its grip on me.

PSALM 101:3

Do not love the world nor the things in the world. If anyone loves the world, the love of the Father is not in him.

1 JOHN 2:15

MOM TO MOM

As your children grow older, they will contend with issues that kids of previous generations either rarely encountered or never dreamed of: exposure to violence, pornography, and explicit language in media and music; an overtly sexualized society; Internet predators and cyberbullies; and easy access to alcohol and illicit drugs. Be encouraged, though— you *can* make a difference! Read reviews of television shows, movies, video games, and music before you watch, rent, or buy. Make time to watch, play, and listen with your kids so you know what they're experiencing. Ask yourself: Does this movie or song reflect our family's faith and values? What hidden messages are my kids learning? Don't be afraid to hit the Off button if the content is inappropriate, and set limits on your children's screen time. Explain your objections so your kids understand your concerns. Your diligence in managing the media's messages to your family today will pay dividends for a lifetime.

ACTION STEPS

1. Before establishing media policies for your family, examine your own behavior. Are you watching or listening to material that is a positive or negative example for your kids? If it's less than positive, make changes now.

2. Talk to your children about the subtle messages in movies, music, and advertising and why they often encourage unhealthy, ungodly attitudes. Talk about how this verse—"Do

not turn to the right nor to the left; turn your foot from evil" (Proverbs 4:27)—applies to media messages.

3. Pray daily for your family's protection from evil influences.

Heavenly Father, I ask You to send angels every day to protect the young lives You have entrusted to us. Shield them from images and ideas that cause harm, Lord, and fill them with Your love, mercy, and grace.

18

role models

I'm always telling my teenagers to treat others with kindness and respect, but too often they are rude and uncooperative instead. Maybe it's because I struggle with this myself?

THE LORD'S SOLUTION

In all things show yourself to be an example of good deeds, with purity in doctrine, dignified, sound in speech which is beyond reproach.

TITUS 2:7–8

Be imitators of me, just as I also am of Christ.

1 CORINTHIANS 11:1

MOM TO MOM

You've probably heard the old saying "Do as I say, not as I do." If only parenting were that easy! We moms know that most of the time, our kids pay much more attention to what we *do* than what we say. Above all else, our actions communicate what we believe and value. That's important to remember as we try to apply the Bible's instruction on childrearing: "Train up a child in the way he should go, even when he is old he will not depart from it" (Proverbs 22:6). If we respond to people and problems with love, kindness, patience, and compassion, we are training our children to do likewise. If our responses most often center on irritation and frustration, we pass on these lessons as well. This also applies to our faith. Kids are so smart. When we demonstrate a genuine love and respect for the Lord, they notice. If we don't, they pick up on that too! Like it or not, we are role models for our families—so let's influence them in ways that are most pleasing to our Father in heaven.

ACTION STEPS

1. Take an honest inventory of your behavior. What messages does it send to the people around you? If you aren't reflecting Jesus in your thoughts and actions, take steps today that will lead to lasting change. You might start by taking the matter to Him in prayer.

2. Who else are role models in your children's lives—friends, teachers, leaders at church? Identify whether these people

are influencing your kids in positive ways. Talk to your children about it, and, if needed, encourage them to seek new role models.

Dear Jesus, thank You for being the ultimate role model. Grant that our ways as parents would match our words. As our children look to us as examples, may they see You.

19

the power of a promise

When my kids pester me with demands, I tend to say I'll buy them something or take them somewhere, just to get them off my back. Then I don't always follow through. Is that really so bad?

THE LORD'S SOLUTION

"You have heard that the ancients were told, 'You shall not make false vows, but shall fulfill your vows to the Lord.' But I say to you, make no oath at all. . . . Let your statement be, 'Yes, yes' or 'No, no'; anything beyond these is of evil."

MATTHEW 5:33–37

MOM TO MOM

As a mom, I understand how easy it is for whining children to frustrate us and cause us to look for quick solutions. When we promise one thing and do another, however, we're laying the groundwork for a much bigger problem: our children will no longer trust what we say and will learn that it's okay to mislead others. Jesus is clear about what our word should mean: "You shall not make false vows" (Matthew 5:33). We know, after all, that we can depend on the promises of the Lord. He holds tomorrow, and His Word is unchanging. He has made covenants with the people of Israel and with us that are everlasting. As Paul wrote, "If we are faithless, He remains faithful, for He cannot deny Himself" (2 Timothy 2:13). If the Lord can keep His Word for eternity, can't we keep our word with our children?

ACTION STEPS

1. Read and reflect on these Scripture verses about God's faithfulness: Deuteronomy 7:8–9; Psalm 36:5; 1 Corinthians 1:9; 2 Peter 3:9. Praise and thank the Lord for His unshakable commitment to us.

2. Make a list of alternative responses for the next time you find yourself facing demands from your kids. Establish boundaries, as well as consequences for inappropriate behavior. Consider this reply: "Yes, you can buy that. It's not in our budget right now, but this is what it costs, and you can

earn the money to buy it yourself." Remember to be consistent. Let your yes be yes and your no, no.

Dear God, You have shown me the power of Your promises. Help me to make my word my bond and to be wise in the way I respond to the needs and wants of my children.

20

the bread of life

I'm having trouble with my twelve-year-old. When he's stressed out, he eats, and now he's gained a lot of weight. I can't figure out what to do.

THE LORD'S SOLUTION

*Do not be wise in your own eyes; fear the L*ORD *and turn away from evil. It will be healing to your body and refreshment to your bones.*

PROVERBS 3:7–8

Jesus said to them, "I am the bread of life; he who comes to Me will not hunger, and he who believes in Me will never thirst."

JOHN 6:35

MOM TO MOM

Researchers estimate that one-third of children in the United States are either overweight or obese. Increasing numbers of these kids are being diagnosed with type 2 diabetes, high blood pressure, bad cholesterol, and other obesity complications. Equally distressing is the growing number of children who suffer from eating disorders such as anorexia. Compulsive eating and anorexia are flip sides of the same coin—both involve unhealthy relationships with food. While the origins of eating disorders are complex, and I don't presume to suggest I have all the answers, I do know this: the temporary pleasure derived from adding or subtracting calories will never fulfill anyone for long. Happiness ultimately derives from a deeper source. For me, that source is my relationship with God. If someone you love is battling an eating disorder, please seek the help you need. A deeper relationship with and trust in the Lord is a great place to start.

ACTION STEPS

1. If you suspect your son or daughter has an eating disorder, it's urgent that you identify and deal with it immediately. Check for symptoms online. Consult a professional counselor. The longer you put it off, the greater the danger to your family.

2. If your kids (or spouse or you) are simply eating too much and exercising too little, make a plan to change your lifestyle.

Can you incorporate more healthy foods into everyone's diet? Can you schedule physical activities that you all enjoy and are likely to continue? It doesn't take much to develop healthy habits that last a lifetime.

Lord Jesus, You are the Bread of Life. Give me the wisdom and ability to help my family enjoy a healthy relationship with food and, most important of all, with You.

21

honor thy parents

Every time my mother comes to visit, we end up in an argument. When she brings up mistakes I made twenty years ago, I find myself responding in kind. Can't I just banish her from my life?

THE LORD'S SOLUTION

Honor your father and your mother, as the LORD your God has commanded you, that your days may be prolonged and that it may go well with you on the land which the LORD your God gives you.

DEUTERONOMY 5:16

MOM TO MOM

It can be terribly discouraging to relive old hurts and wounds with family members. I empathize with anyone who is dealing with this issue today. I also know that it is so important that we honor our elders, especially our parents. Though I am blessed with a loving relationship with my mom and dad, I realize that's not the case for so many. As difficult as it seems, I urge you to return harsh or critical words with respect. If we don't, how can we expect our children to honor us? The apostle Paul also points out that the commandment to honor father and mother comes with a promise: "that it may be well with you, and that you may live long on the earth" (Ephesians 6:2–3). My prayer is that it may be well with you as you seek restored and loving family relationships.

ACTION STEPS

1. If you have difficult interactions with your parents, look for ways to minimize your differences. Perhaps you can agree to disagree when resolutions aren't possible.

2. I have friends who have challenging relationships with their parents, yet they've still found ways to love and forgive them. Try to understand the reasons behind your parents' critical attitudes. When you do, you may find the forgiveness demonstrated by our Lord flows just a little bit easier.

3. If parental visits continue to cause unceasing stress in your life, the next time the suggestion comes up, let them

know—with love and respect—that you need more time with your immediate family.

Father, it is sometimes much easier to love You than my parents here on earth! Fill my heart with love and grace so that in every circumstance I may offer my parents the genuine honor and respect You ask of me.

22

holy holidays

I'm so focused during the holidays on decorating, getting ready to host my extended family, and the mad scramble of last-minute shopping that I barely remember what we're celebrating. Help!

THE LORD'S SOLUTION

Holy, Holy, Holy, is the LORD of hosts, the whole earth is full of His glory.

ISAIAH 6:3

The angel said to them, "Do not be afraid; for behold, I bring you good news of great joy which will be for all the people; for today in the city of David there has been born for you a Savior, who is Christ the Lord."

LUKE 2:10–11

MOM TO MOM

If the meaning of the season has passed you by, it's time to stop and breathe. Remember, the holidays are *holy* days. Set aside some time to investigate and reflect on your faith traditions and the beliefs they represent. If you're not sure about the messages behind those traditions, do the research (the internet is a great tool) so you *do* understand. In our family, the holidays are about celebrating the birth of our loving Savior, Jesus, and the gift of eternal life He represents. Your holidays should be a time of joy. Don't let busyness, shopping, and striving to get everything "just right" overshadow the reason for the season. Material gifts mean less than a phone call, a hug, or an unexpected visit to a friend or loved one. When you spread the Lord's love and honor your faith, you'll rediscover the joy and meaning of your holiday celebrations.

ACTION STEPS

1. Make a list of everything you're trying to accomplish this holiday season. Now ask yourself how many items on the list are truly necessary. Cross out the ones that aren't. Learn to "let go and let God."

2. Read about the birth of Jesus in the first two chapters of the book of Luke. It will help you put your holidays back into perspective.

Slow me down, dear Lord. Change my pace and my heart so that I may rediscover Your love and holiness, not only this holiday season, but every day of my life.

23

a name above every name

My friend believes in God, but she refuses to accept the divinity of Jesus and has yet to invite Him into her heart. I don't want to offend or upset her, so I find myself avoiding the name of Jesus altogether.

THE LORD'S SOLUTION

God highly exalted Him, and bestowed on Him the name which is above every name, so that at the name of Jesus every knee will bow, of those who are in heaven and on earth and under the earth, and that every tongue will confess that Jesus Christ is Lord, to the glory of God the Father.

PHILIPPIANS 2:9–11

MOM TO MOM

Nothing gets our attention like hearing our name. When someone we met long ago remembers our name when we meet again, we feel honored. When a child or spouse speaks our name with great affection, it can melt our hearts. This applies just as much when we speak the name of our Savior. *Jesus* is a holy name, and when we use it in a spirit of reverence and love, we offer Him praise. Though most people believe in God in one form or another, the name of His Son is controversial to some. In this age of political correctness, however, Jesus does not call us to be timid or ashamed of Him. He deeply desires that His children know the truth about who He is. Though, of course, we must respect others' feelings, we should never be afraid to worship and praise our Lord and shout His name to the world.

ACTION STEPS

1. Read these verses of Scripture: Matthew 1:21, 18:20; Mark 9:37–39; John 14:13–14; Acts 4:12; Romans 10:13. What do they tell you about the power of the name of Jesus?

2. Talk with your family about the power of names—in particular, the power of the name of our Lord.

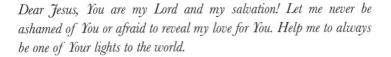

Dear Jesus, You are my Lord and my salvation! Let me never be ashamed of You or afraid to reveal my love for You. Help me to always be one of Your lights to the world.

24

not rules, but relationship

I go to church each Sunday and try to live by biblical principles, yet something is missing. I feel like I'm just going through the motions. What's wrong with my faith?

THE LORD'S SOLUTION

Behold, I stand at the door and knock; if anyone hears my voice and opens the door, I will come in to him and will dine with him, and he with Me.

REVELATION 3:20

MOM TO MOM

In our "go, go, go" society, it's easy for us to turn our spiritual lives into lists of things to do. Faith, however, is about much more than getting into a routine of going to church or following rules. It's real. It's personal. It's a *relationship*. Scripture tells us to "Draw near to God and He will draw near to you" (James 4:8). If you are genuinely seeking Him in your heart, you will indeed feel His presence. How? When He speaks to you through His Word. When He answers your prayers by opening or closing the door on opportunities. When He encourages you through the words and actions of others. Jesus is the focus and first love of my life. Though my faith is still growing, He brings such comfort, peace, purpose, and joy to me and my loved ones. I believe you'll discover renewed faith and joy when you go deeper in your relationship with the Savior.

ACTION STEPS

1. Memorize the Scripture passage from Revelation 3:20 above. Reflect on how this verse applies to you. Is Jesus knocking on the door of your life? Are you letting Him in?

2. Set aside at least thirty minutes to pray to the Lord. Talk to Him as you would a friend—after all, He is the "friend who sticks closer than a brother" (Proverbs 18:24).

Oh Lord, I so often focus on rules and routines instead of my relationship with You. My soul longs for Your presence! Forgive me for my foolishness, and help me to again draw near to You.

25

royalty in His kingdom

My ten-year-old daughter is having a rough time—other kids tease her, and she's struggling with schoolwork. I see her self-esteem slipping and don't know what to do about it.

THE LORD'S SOLUTION

You are a chosen race, a royal priesthood, a holy nation, a people for God's own possession.

1 PETER 2:9

We are His workmanship, created in Christ Jesus for good works.

EPHESIANS 2:10

MOM TO MOM

At different moments in their lives, each of our daughters, Lily and Chloe, deeply enjoyed princesses and princess stories. They also each sadly concluded that they could never be "real" princesses. It was an opportunity for me to remind them of their value. I told each of them, "Oh, but you already are a princess, darling. You are the ultimate princess because your Father in heaven is the King of kings." Every little girl is a princess in God's kingdom, and every little boy is an ambassador and warrior for the Lord. In His eyes, they are royalty, deserving of the greatest respect and love. If we teach our children this concept when they are young and treat them accordingly, they will grow up with a strong foundation, one that won't be easily shaken during life's hard moments. Of course your children will still face discouraging circumstances. When they do, remind them of their status as royalty—and that they can always depend on the King of kings.

ACTION STEPS

1. Are you doing all you can to show your children that you're on their team? Make it a point this week to ask how they're doing, listen to their answers, and encourage them with their struggles.

2. Read Psalm 139 with your family—"I am fearfully and wonderfully made" (v. 14)—and talk about what that means for your children (and for you).

Heavenly Father, we are so grateful to be members of Your holy family. Please enable my precious children to view themselves as You see them—as royalty in Your holy kingdom.

26

keep listening

I'm so focused on getting through each day that I feel like I'm missing out on God's plan for my life. It's like He's speaking to me and I just can't hear Him.

THE LORD'S SOLUTION

When you are in distress and all these things have come upon you, in the latter days you will return to the LORD your God and listen to His voice.

DEUTERONOMY 4:30

Guard your steps as you go to the house of God and draw near to listen.

ECCLESIASTES 5:1

MOM TO MOM

Isn't it amazing that God values us so much that He asks us
to play a role in His purposes? He is the Creator of the uni-
verse. God doesn't need us, yet He invites us to carry out His
perfect plans. Do you know the passage of Scripture that
says, "Today if you hear His voice, do not harden your
hearts" (Hebrews 3:15)? Stop. Breathe. Open your eyes,
your ears, and your heart—on this very day, the Lord is call-
ing on you to participate in His wonderful plan for the
future. His voice can be found in the simple joy of a sunrise,
a flower, or a cloud. Every good thing, even each breath we
take, is a gift from the Lord and a call to fulfill our God-
designed destiny. Slow down, keep on listening, and you'll
rediscover the holy voice we all long to hear.

ACTION STEPS

1. Set aside at least a half hour of quiet time daily. Ask the
Lord about His plan for your future, then stop and do nothing except listen for His answer. Sometimes all it takes to
hear the Lord's voice is giving Him the time to speak.

2. Do you ever receive—and ignore—a "holy nudge" from
heaven? Is it possible that God is speaking to you and you
don't like what you're hearing? Open your heart to anything
and everything the Lord is telling you, and be ready to act
on it.

Dear Lord, I am truly thankful that You have a plan for my life and that You are always ready to communicate the next step to me—even when I'm not ready to hear it. Don't let me harden my heart, Lord! Give me the ears to hear every time You call.

27

insist on integrity

The other night, my ten-year-old told me his home-work was done, but I found out he actually finished it the next day at school. My friend says a little white lie is no big deal, but I'm upset about it.

THE LORD'S SOLUTION

He who walks in integrity walks securely.

PROVERBS 10:9

Till I die I will not put away my integrity from me.

JOB 27:5

MOM TO MOM

The phrase "a little white lie" makes me crazy. Think about that, and I'm sure you'll agree there's no such thing. What is its opposite, a big black lie? Let's not color our lies. Make it clear to your children that the line between honesty and dishonesty is a boundary they don't want to cross, and spell out what will happen if they do. If your kids believe it's no big deal to pass on a few untruths now, it will be far too easy for them to fall into a consistent pattern of lies later. Integrity is the foundation of effective communication, not only within your family but in every interaction in life. Even more important, it brings pleasure to our Lord: "I know, O my God, that You try the heart and delight in uprightness" (1 Chronicles 29:17).

ACTION STEPS

1. Have a meeting with your children. Ask them about times when their friends have lied or when they themselves feel tempted to lie. Explain your position and God's position—and the consequences that result from not telling the truth. Challenge them to be an example for their friends: "In speech, conduct, love, faith and purity, show yourself an example of those who believe" (1 Timothy 4:12).

2. Take the issue of integrity to the Lord in prayer. Ask Him for guidance on dealing with your children—and for insight into any areas in your own life where your integrity falls short of God's design.

Dear Lord, I want to come before You with righteousness and integrity. Help me to avoid dishonest shortcuts and show me how to respond with wisdom when my children fail to live up to Your holy example.

28

the power of forgiveness

The mother of one of my daughter's friends, someone I've considered a good friend, recently insulted me in front of a group of moms. I'm so upset that I can't stop thinking about it!

THE LORD'S SOLUTION

Jesus said to him, "I do not say to you, [forgive] up to seven times, but up to seventy times seven."

MATTHEW 18:22

Just as the Lord forgave you, so also should you.

COLOSSIANS 3:13

MOM TO MOM

We all face situations where others hurt or disappoint us. We need to deal with those issues but not dwell on them. I don't mean that they should be swept under the carpet. If the people involved are family members or friends we want to continue relationships with, we may need to meet with them to resolve any hurt feelings. Working through painful experiences takes time and effort. Yet if we honestly confront any wrongs we've suffered and can forgive—not condone but forgive—the people responsible, we'll be free from bitterness and can look ahead to a brighter future. God has something to say about this too: "Forgive, if you have anything against anyone, so that your Father who is in heaven will also forgive you your transgressions" (Mark 11:25). Though it's certainly not easy, if God can forgive and forget, we can do the same.

ACTION STEPS

1. Do you struggle with bitterness, anger, resentment, depression, health problems, isolation, or addiction? If so, could the cause be that you are withholding forgiveness from someone? Search your heart and see if there is someone you need to forgive. It will benefit you even more than them.

2. When was the last time you honestly confessed your mistakes to the Lord and asked Him to forgive you? If it wasn't today, stop right now and meet Him in prayer.

Dear God, You have forgiven more than I can imagine—and now You ask me to forgive those who hurt me. Thank You for your loving example. Please teach me the healing power of forgiveness.

29

restoring rest

I have three children between the ages of six and twelve, and our afternoons are total chaos. After an hour of phone calls, loud music, and bouncing off the furniture, I either hide in my bedroom or end up snapping at the kids. What's a better way?

THE LORD'S SOLUTION

The LORD lift up His countenance on you, and give you peace.

NUMBERS 6:26

MOM TO MOM

A little loud and crazy "unwind time" after school is a welcome change of pace for many kids; just don't let it dominate the rest of your family's day. Remember, you are the parent! Your children also need moments of peace to rest and recharge. If you sense that the energy level is about to shoot off the scale, then think about ways you can bring it down to a manageable point. It might be time for the kids to start on their homework. Maybe they need to retreat to their rooms to read, listen to a recorded story, or have a quiet prayer time with God. Or you might apply a lesson I learned from a cartoon character. Maybe you've seen the Tasmanian Devil spin into a one-creature wrecking crew? Yet when Bugs Bunny pulls out a violin and performs a sweet lullaby, "Taz" just melts. It's hard to scream, argue, or throw a tantrum when a soothing song is playing. Give it a try.

ACTION STEPS

1. Think about other ways you can insert moments of peace into your children's lives. In our family, for example, we ask our kids to turn off video games and cell phones on our drive to school so we can talk, pray, play games, and encourage each other. Do what works for you.

2. Let Jesus be an example for your family—you need quiet time to rest and pray. If even He "would often slip away to the wilderness and pray" (Luke 5:16) during His incredible

ministry, then we need to give ourselves opportunities to do the same.

Lord, I realize I need more and more of You—Your perspective, Your power, and Your peace. Help us to provide refreshing times for our children that they may use to grow closer to You.

30

what if I blow it?

I'm just starting out as a parent—my oldest is three years old—and I'm so afraid of blowing it. I've made many mistakes in my life. What if I fail as a mom?

THE LORD'S SOLUTION

Give instruction to a wise man and he will be still wiser.

PROVERBS 9:9

The righteous are bold as a lion.

PROVERBS 28:1

MOM TO MOM

We all have an inner critic, that negative voice that constantly reminds us of past mistakes and tells us we're a failure. And guess what? We *will* make mistakes with our children. However, a mistake stays a mistake only if we don't learn from it. Successful people—and parents—turn failures into growth. They say, "Okay, that didn't work. What can I change that will give me a better result next time?" Your love and perseverance is more than enough to make up for a few errors in judgment. Don't let your past hold you back. Believe that you are God's choice to be the mother of your kids. No one is better suited for the role than you.

ACTION STEPS

1. List a few recent mistakes you've made as a mother (don't go overboard—a short list is enough!). Now think about what went wrong in those situations. What do you have the power to change? Decide on steps you can take right now that will help you grow as a mom.

2. Find a quiet moment to meditate on this verse: "Do not throw away your confidence, which has a great reward. For you have need of endurance, so that when you have done the will of God, you may receive what was promised" (Hebrews 10:35–36). Are you confident in the power and sovereignty of God? Take your concerns to Him in prayer.

Heavenly Father, thank You for my children! I ask for confidence in my role as mom to my kids, and for Your guidance each day. Help me to stay hopeful when I fail and to learn from my mistakes.

31

I'm sorry

My daughter was pestering me the other day, and I overreacted by sending her to her room. I feel like I should apologize, but won't that undermine my authority?

THE LORD'S SOLUTION

If we confess our sins, He is faithful and righteous to forgive us our sins and to cleanse us from all unrighteousness.

1 JOHN 1:9

Be kind to one another, tender-hearted, forgiving each other, just as God in Christ also has forgiven you.

EPHESIANS 4:32

MOM TO MOM

No matter how careful we are as parents, and no matter how many parenting books we read, there will be times when we're just wrong. We all make mistakes. Perhaps you'll give your child an unreasonable grounding, or your bad day at work will translate into an angry response at home. When you make those mistakes, don't be afraid to apologize and ask for forgiveness. A genuine "I'm sorry" won't undermine your authority—instead, it will show that you are confident enough to admit your errors. Your children will appreciate your honesty, and they'll learn that an apology is the best follow-up to a mistake. They'll also be encouraged to know that you plan to do better next time. My experience is that families who are willing to admit their mistakes live in the happiest homes.

ACTION STEPS

1. When you apologize to your children for a mistake, make sure it's from the heart—they will see right through an insincere confession. Before you talk with your kids, ask yourself: *What do I really mean by "I'm sorry"? How will I express it? How will I continue to live it?*

2. Reflect on humility and how it relates to your willingness to admit mistakes. Read what Scripture has to say about humility (see Psalm 18:27, 25:9; Matthew 23:12; Ephesians 4:2; James 4:10).

Lord Jesus, it's never easy to admit that I'm wrong, especially to my children. Give me the courage to seek forgiveness from my kids when I fail. Help us to establish Your solid foundations for a happy home.

32

life without limits

I feel trapped by the constant obstacles I face. If it's not my health or challenges with my kids, it's financial pressures and issues at work. When will I move past all this and get my life back?

THE LORD'S SOLUTION

I am well content with weaknesses, with insults, with distresses, with persecutions, with difficulties, for Christ's sake; for when I am weak, then I am strong.

2 CORINTHIANS 12:10

MOM TO MOM

I do understand the burdens so many moms bear every day, often every minute. When challenges begin to stack one on top of the other, they can look like a skyscraper that's ready to topple. When obstacles threaten to overwhelm you, I suggest that you ask yourself a couple of key questions: *Is the Lord letting me confront these issues for a reason? And am I allowing Him to shine through my problems?* The apostle Paul had an unknown physical ailment; three times he asked the Lord to remove it. The Lord's answer? "My grace is sufficient for you, for power is perfected in weakness" (2 Corinthians 12:9). I think of my friend Nick Vujicic as a modern-day Paul. He was born without arms or legs, yet today he is an author, pastor, and motivational speaker who travels around the world inspiring people with his message about the love and hope found in Jesus. His is a life without limits. Yours can be too.

ACTION STEPS

1. Pull out your journal or laptop and write down your thoughts about Jesus's statement "Power is perfected in weakness." What do you think He is saying?

2. Make a list of your most difficult challenges, then write down how God is—or could be, with a few changes on your part—seen by others as working in those circumstances. Pray for wisdom on how to handle your obstacles.

Dear Jesus, I know that there are no limits to Your power and grace. Take away the problems that are too much for me, and show me how to accept and embrace the trials that will glorify You.

33

dealing with crisis

I'm so upset I could scream. We've talked with our kids many times about the dangers of sex before marriage. I thought our message was getting through, but now my sixteen-year-old daughter is pregnant. I don't think I can handle this!

THE LORD'S SOLUTION

Encourage one another and build up one another.

1 THESSALONIANS 5:11

The lips of the righteous feed many.

PROVERBS 10:21

MOM TO MOM

Despite all of our prayers and heartfelt warnings, our children will make mistakes, some with lifelong consequences. Your daughter or your son's girlfriend may be pregnant; your daughter may have caused a terrible car accident; your son may have stolen a stereo system. Whatever the crisis, accusations and angry words on your part will only make matters worse. In moments like these, your child desperately needs your support and guidance. Give everyone time to control their emotions, then talk calmly about what's happened and what the options are for dealing with it. Most important of all, let your son or daughter know that you are on the same team, that you forgive them, and will stand by them no matter what—and that God will do the same. Your loving response in a crisis may be the greatest lesson you will ever pass on to your children.

ACTION STEPS

1. Think back to some of the crisis moments in your life. How did the people around you respond? How did they help or hurt you and your situation? How do you wish they'd responded?

2. Read John 4:7–30, the story of Jesus and the woman at the well. How did Jesus demonstrate love and mercy even while encouraging the woman to put an end to her sin? How can this be an example for us as we raise our children?

Dear Lord, I pray that You will protect my children from harm and unwise choices. I also ask that You give me the strength to respond with love and wisdom when they make mistakes. Let me always follow You and Your example, no matter what.

34

possession obsession

I love to shop. My house is filled with clothes, jewelry, and other things I was sure I needed at the time. Now it feels like a waste. I'm surrounded by "stuff." What's wrong with me?

THE LORD'S SOLUTION

Do not be afraid when a man grows rich, . . . for when he dies he will carry nothing away.

PSALM 49:16–17

Do not store up for yourselves treasures on earth, where moth and rust destroy, and where thieves break in and steal. But store up for yourselves treasures in heaven; . . . for where your treasure is, there your heart will be also.

MATTHEW 6:19–21

MOM TO MOM

"Possession obsession" is a common affliction. When we see a diamond necklace advertised on television or a new RV parked in our neighbor's driveway, we may start buying into the idea that we deserve the best, whether we can afford it or not. Yet the minute we adopt a sense of entitlement—a feeling that if "everyone else" has something, we should have it too—we've fallen into a trap. Material things cannot make us happy. That's what Jesus was talking about when He said, "A man's life does not consist in the abundance of his possessions" (Luke 12:15 NIV). Take an honest look at your attitude toward possessions and money. If you're making financial decisions based on the idea that you deserve something, you may be taking your family on the road to possession obsession. Please turn around before you drive off a cliff. If you ruthlessly evaluate each potential purchase and make your decision based on need rather than a feeling of entitlement, you'll be heading in the right direction.

ACTION STEPS

1. Look at your possessions. How many are truly worth their price? Remember that you give up not only financial resources when you make a purchase, but also the time it will take to clean, maintain, and protect it. Today, identify and get rid of a few items you can live without, and notice the freedom it gives you.

2. Read the parable of the rich fool in Luke 12:13–21. What is Jesus telling us here?

Dear Jesus, I am so easily distracted by the desire to own more things. Help me to let go of what I do not need and see what truly has lasting value.

35

having it all

I have everything I ever wanted—a great husband, family, career, and home, plus I sing with the worship team at church—but the truth is that I'm miserable. I don't know what I'm doing or where I'm going. It's too much!

THE LORD'S SOLUTION

I have inherited Your testimonies forever, for they are the joy of my heart.

PSALM 119:111

A scribe came and said to [Jesus], "Teacher, I will follow You wherever You go."

MATTHEW 8:19

MOM TO MOM

I once made the statement that women can "have it all," but that we may not be able to have it all at the same time. Marriage, career, motherhood, household CEO, commitments to church and other nonprofit organizations, and other life responsibilities are enormous challenges that will drain anyone. Trying to fill all of these roles successfully as well as simultaneously is like juggling three balls while riding a bicycle across a tightrope over Niagara Falls. You *might* be able to pull it off, but it's more likely that sooner or later, something—probably you—will be going over the edge! Are you trying to be everything to everyone because it brings you happiness or because it's part of someone else's agenda? Don't substitute another person's definition of a successful, happy life for yours. For me, joy comes from following the path I believe God has set me on. Define your vision of success, then take steps to start living it.

ACTION STEPS

1. What does success mean to you? Put aside your ideas of what others might say and write down a definition that makes sense for you and your life. Now ask yourself what needs to happen to move you closer to your version of success.

2. How do you think God defines success? Write that down too. Include verses from Scripture that you believe apply. Take some time to reflect on what you've written, then take it to the Lord in prayer.

Heavenly Father, I do confess that I get caught up in the expectations of the world and other people. Help me to put You and Your will above everything else so that I will be a success in Your eyes.

36

celebrate your family's gifts

We've always encouraged our son, now thirteen, to do his best on homework, and he's excelled in school. We've done the same with our daughter, now eleven, yet she struggles with every school assignment. What did we do wrong?

THE LORD'S SOLUTION

Before I formed you in the womb I knew you, before you were born I set you apart.

JEREMIAH 1:5 (NIV)

He who began a good work in you will perfect it until the day of Christ Jesus.

PHILIPPIANS 1:6

MOM TO MOM

If your kids are trying hard and still do not excel, it may be no one's fault. Understand that each son or daughter is an individual with specific, God-given gifts and traits. Pay attention to your kids' unique abilities and characteristics. Help them recognize these qualities in themselves and commend your children when they demonstrate their talents. If your son has an aptitude for math, let him know how pleased and impressed you are with his work. If your daughter struggles in the classroom but has a knack for playing the saxophone, encourage her to develop her music skills. Your support will help your kids feel better about themselves and enable them to see their differences not as faults but as special, valued gifts. Keep in mind that you and your husband are also unique individuals. If you begin to see his weaknesses as problems or obstacles, remember that your varying abilities are what make you a strong team. When we celebrate our strengths—and our differences—we are more powerful and effective members of God's family.

ACTION STEPS

1. Make a list of each of your children's gifts. Do they have other talents you haven't fully explored yet? Look for new ways to encourage your kids to develop their God-given abilities.

2. I don't mean to imply that academics or the ability to balance a checkbook are insignificant. If your son or daughter

isn't gifted in an important area, consider ways to support him or her. Can you take more time to help with homework? Could you hire a friend or tutor? Work with teachers and others to find a solution.

Dear God, You have blessed each of our family members in unique ways. Give us discernment to support each other in our weaknesses and to encourage each other to use our gifts fully for Your glory.

37

no exceptions

I've made terrible mistakes in my life, including an affair and an abortion. I live with guilt and regret every day. My kids both follow Jesus, and I believe they'll be in heaven one day, but after what I've done, I have no hope of joining them.

THE LORD'S SOLUTION

All sins shall be forgiven the sons of men, and whatever blasphemies they utter.

MARK 3:28

The sorrow that is according to the will of God produces a repentance without regret, leading to salvation.

2 CORINTHIANS 7:10

MOM TO MOM

Is anything sadder—or more unnecessary—than a life of regret? It's so important for us to understand that *no* sin is too great for the Lord's forgiveness! If anyone had reason to regret his life, it was the apostle Paul. He watched and probably encouraged the murder of Stephen. He persecuted Christians at every turn. Yet when Jesus brought him to his knees, Paul had the wisdom to not only accept the Lord's offer of complete and unconditional forgiveness, but also fully forgive himself for his poor choices. If Paul can do that, so can you. When you reveal your sins to Jesus, express genuine sorrow, and ask Him to forgive you. He will—no exceptions: "If we confess our sins, He is faithful and righteous to forgive us our sins and to cleanse us from all unrighteousness" (1 John 1:9). When He does, we can trust that those sins are forgotten. They are as far from us as "the east is from the west" (Psalm 103:12). That's a long way!

ACTION STEPS

1. Because of guilt, some of us don't believe we deserve God's forgiveness. We'd rather punish ourselves than have our slate wiped clean. Yet His call to repentance isn't just a suggestion—He insists (see Acts 3:19). If this is your situation, don't disobey a moment longer. Ask Jesus for forgiveness *right now*.

2. Have you received the Lord's forgiveness but are still playing mental tapes of past mistakes? The next time one of

those tapes begins, hit Stop and Erase in your mind. It's time to let go of the past, live in the present, and look forward to the future God has designed for you.

Lord Jesus, I am so sorry for my life of sin and for holding on to guilt and regret! Please forgive me today, show me how to forget the past, and enable me to begin anew, walking in step with You.

38

God's map

I've accepted Jesus as my Savior, and I attend church. I read the Bible before making the decision to give my life to Christ, but now I'm so busy. I'm going to heaven anyway, so does Bible study really matter?

THE LORD'S SOLUTION

This book of the law shall not depart from your mouth, but you shall meditate on it day and night.

JOSHUA 1:8

Your word is a lamp to my feet and a light to my path.

PSALM 119:105

MOM TO MOM

Suppose you're heading out on a two-week hiking trip in the wilderness. You'll want to be prepared, so your "must bring" list will include food, water, hiking boots, a tent, and a sleeping bag. I'm guessing that a map will be on your list too. Without it, you'll soon be lost, right? Well, the Bible is our map to the life of faith God wants us to lead—and without it, we'll surely get lost. Everything we need to know about our Creator, our purpose, and where we're going is contained in those pages. It tells us about the good paths to take and the dangers to avoid. It tells the stories of people who reached their heavenly destinations and of others who got tragically off track. Paul wrote, "All Scripture is inspired by God and profitable for teaching, for reproof, for correction, for training in righteousness" (2 Timothy 3:16). That's the kind of powerful map we all need if we're going to keep our bearings in the "wilderness" of today's world.

ACTION STEPS

1. Read Psalm 119. What does it say about how we as believers should regard the Word of God? Write down the benefits listed in this psalm of meditating on God's law, as well as the drawbacks if we don't.

2. Look at your habits and schedule, and make a plan to include daily Bible reading and reflection, starting today.

Dear God, I realize that Your Word is essential to my joy and Your good plan for my life. Guide me in making changes so that I can spend more time with You and Your map for me.

39

true friends

My only close friend recently moved out of state, and I miss her terribly. We just clicked. Now I don't feel I have the energy to start over and develop a new friendship.

THE LORD'S SOLUTION

A friend loves at all times, and a brother is born for adversity.

PROVERBS 17:17

There is a friend who sticks closer than a brother.

PROVERBS 18:24

MOM TO MOM

It can be scary and intimidating to initiate reaching out to others in friendship, yet the rewards make the effort more than worth it. A true friend is someone who will lovingly listen, build you up, provide constructive criticism, and offer a shoulder to cry on. A friend will encourage you to reach for your dreams. When we started our business with a line of designer socks, John and Marilyn Moretz were our first brand partners. They believed in us and our vision and gave us wings to fly. A friend who is a sister or brother in Christ will support you and spur you on as you grow deeper in your faith. I am so grateful for the friends in our life; they are like angels of wisdom and protection. As difficult as it seems, please persevere in seeking out fellowship with others. As you do, remember to lean on the one true Friend who will always love you, listen to you, and be there for you: Jesus.

ACTION STEPS

1. If you have trouble making friends, start small. Introduce yourself to someone you might like to know. Later, you can invite that person out to coffee or lunch.

2. To meet new people, sign up for a women's Bible study, class, or book club.

3. Remember that relationships take time to form, so don't feel you have to make a close friend in a single day. Scripture says that "Godly people are careful about the friends they

choose" (Proverbs 12:26 NIrv). Trust your intuition, and let Jesus be your guide.

Dear Jesus, I know that friends and fellowship are part of Your plan for my life. Help me to be the kind of friend I seek—loving, encouraging, and always faithful to You.

40

it's okay to say no

Every time someone asks me to volunteer on a church project or school fundraiser, I say yes. Now my schedule is completely overbooked. Yet I feel so guilty when I can't help out. What's the answer?

THE LORD'S SOLUTION

Train the younger women to love their husbands and children, to be self-controlled and pure, to be busy at home.

TITUS 2:4–5 (NIV)

I want you to be wise in what is good.

ROMANS 16:19

MOM TO MOM

Setting boundaries for your family, and for yourself, is essential if you are going to live a life of excellence. God created women to be helpers and nurturers, and it feels right to fulfill that role. If your helping leaves you so exhausted and cranky that no one wants to be around you, however, how much "help" are you really providing? There's no need to feel guilty over setting limits. Remember, anytime you add an activity to your schedule, you're taking away from something else. It's more than okay to say no to someone else's request if it doesn't line up with your priorities. Yes, the Lord instructs us to help and encourage others. He also wants us to be wise in the way we allocate our energy and time: "Blessed is the man who finds wisdom. . . . She [wisdom] is more precious than jewels" (Proverbs 3:13, 15).

ACTION STEPS

1. When I'm at home, I screen my phone calls. Even people I love have to go to voice mail. I get back to them, just not necessarily on their timetable. That's a boundary that works for me. Think about new boundaries you can set that will give you freedom and peace of mind.

2. The Lord does not want us to live with guilt. Have you truly offended Him by saying no to someone? If so, confess your mistake, accept His forgiveness, and move on. If not, let go of your guilt, and recognize that boundaries bring peace.

Heavenly Father, I desperately need Your guidance for my life. Help me to find the right balance between helping others and taking care of myself and my family.

41

dreams and destiny

I used to be excited about the future. I had ideas about starting my own craft business and working with young people. Now I feel like life is pressing me down. I can't see beyond the next day, let alone the future.

THE LORD'S SOLUTION

"I know the plans I have for you," declares the LORD, "plans to prosper you and not to harm you, plans to give you hope and a future."

JEREMIAH 29:11 (NIV)

Delight yourself in the LORD; and He will give you the desires of your heart.

PSALM 37:4

MOM TO MOM

When you were young, did you dream about what you wanted to be when you grew up? I know I did. I wanted to be a newspaper reporter, a marine biologist, and a teacher. Our dreams are part of the process of discovering the person we were born to be. They are glimpses into the future, where we look beyond who we are into the mist of what we might become. Most moms enter marriage with high hopes and dreams, but the daily responsibility of managing a household and caring for a husband and children can weigh them down to the point that dreams disappear. Just as you did as a child, you still need to dream! God gave you abilities and passions because He has a purpose for your life. Pursuing dreams and goals can lead you to that purpose. Though faith and family should remain the priorities, please don't let go of your dreams. They are windows into your destiny.

ACTION STEPS

1. What are your dreams for yourself, your marriage, your family, and your career? What do you want each of those areas to look like next month, next year, in five years, and ten years from now? What is holding you back? Begin removing the obstacles today, and start reaching for your dreams.

2. Abraham Lincoln endured twenty-seven years of disappointments and rejections before becoming president of the

United States. Think about your own disappointments and rejections. What did you gain from those experiences? Give yourself the freedom to fail—and to grow—as you pursue your dreams.

Lord, it is such a comfort to know You want to give me hope and a future. Please show me the steps that will lead me to Your purpose for my life, starting today.

42

helping the hurting

Today, I saw an elderly woman in our neighborhood struggling to bring in her groceries. She seemed so sad. I could have stopped to help, but I was late for an appointment. It's bothered me ever since.

THE LORD'S SOLUTION

If there is any encouragement in Christ, if there is any consolations of love . . . make my joy complete by being of the same mind, maintaining the same love.

PHILIPPIANS 2:1–2

You shall love your neighbor as yourself.

MARK 12:31

MOM TO MOM

We live in a world of hurting people. Many are struggling with finances, with their health, and with emotional burdens. When we see beyond ourselves and observe the needs of the people around us, we open ourselves up to all kinds of opportunities for joy. Years ago I worked in a convalescent home. It was a pleasure to deliver meals to the elderly patients, many of whom had no one else to visit them. The simple acts of giving them a hug and a meal brought smiles to their faces and happiness to my heart. Of course, many more people are hurting today—from young children to men and women at the end of their lives—because they have no hope in Jesus. When we reach out to someone and invite them to discover a relationship with Him, we can lead them to the greatest gift of all. That brings on a special joy that can't be surpassed—welcoming a new member into the family of God!

ACTION STEPS

1. Who do you know in your neighborhood, at work, or in your church who might need a little encouragement this week? Make a plan to do something about it.

2. Think about ways to demonstrate compassion in front of your kids. Better yet, invite them to join you. Your children will receive a powerful lesson on love if you allow them to participate in spreading the joy of Jesus.

Dear Jesus, You are the perfect example of compassion. Show me how to be more like You as I reach out to others and share about the wonderful life You offer to all.

43

the lifeline of prayer

When I invited the Lord into my heart, I felt a closeness to Him that I cherished. But these days I feel disconnected from Him. I have to admit that I don't spend as much time with Him as I once did. Is that what's wrong?

THE LORD'S SOLUTION

Pray without ceasing; in everything give thanks; for this is God's will for you in Christ Jesus.

1 THESSALONIANS 5:17–18

At all times they ought to pray and not to lose heart.

LUKE 18:1

MOM TO MOM

A living faith in God is about more than believing in Him, going to church, or even reading the Bible. It's an ongoing relationship, and that takes communication. It's important to schedule times to pray and to listen to His voice. That's what a relationship is—talking and listening. For me, what works is setting my alarm clock early enough that I can start my day with Him. You may find other times that work better for you—maybe during a break time at home or the office or just before going to bed. The main thing is to keep the lines of communication open. Our Lord wants to hear from you about your joys and sorrows. No problem is too big or too small to take to Him. Please don't underestimate the power of prayer. It's our lifeline to our Father in heaven, and it's always available to us.

ACTION STEPS

1. I've found that God sometimes nudges me to pray at times that don't fit my schedule. I've tried to be faithful in obeying those nudges. Are you being faithful to "holy nudges"? The next time you sense one, try putting aside whatever you're doing to focus on Him.

2. In a similar way, the Lord sometimes encourages us to pray for someone who is giving us grief. Ask Jesus right now if there is anyone you should be praying for, even if it's someone you'd rather forget about. Your prayers may be desperately needed.

Dear God, I am so grateful that I can talk to You in prayer! Our holy conversations help me know You better, hear You more clearly, and love my family more deeply.

44

declaration of dependence

I've always been an independent person. I recently invited Christ into my heart, but I often still find myself doing my own thing. What's that about?

THE LORD'S SOLUTION

As for me, the nearness of God is my good; I have made the Lord GOD my refuge, that I may tell of all Your works.

PSALM 73:28

If we live, we live for the Lord, or if we die, we die for the Lord; therefore whether we live or die, we are the Lord's.

ROMANS 14:8

MOM TO MOM

Most of us have an independent streak in us. We want to do things our way. We don't like to ask for help or be dependent on someone else. Sooner or later, though, we all run into situations that are too messy and overwhelming to handle by ourselves. Guess what? Those situations are going to keep coming. God designed our lives that way so we would learn to depend on Him. I've found that the more time I spend with the Lord, the more I realize how much I need Him. Some people see that as weakness. They call it using a crutch. I admit it—I want and desperately need God's love and support as I walk through life. When I try to handle things on my own, I mess up. Our Lord is more than a friend who rescues us in times of need. He is our daily source of power and love. The secret of life is to love and depend on Him—for everything.

ACTION STEPS

1. In what circumstances are you most likely to fend for yourself and resist help from anyone? The next time you face that situation, what could you do differently so that you turn first to the Lord?

2. Read Ecclesiastes 4:9–12. What is Solomon saying about people who try to go through life on their own?

3. Write out a personal "declaration of dependence," and dedicate it to the Lord.

Lord, I am so thankful that You desire to be a powerful presence in my life. Enable me to always remember to love and depend on You.

45

passing on the faith

My husband and I are believers, and of course we want our children (now four and two) to follow us in our faith. When is the time to start introducing them to Jesus, and how?

THE LORD'S SOLUTION

I have no greater joy than this, to hear of my children walking in the truth.

3 JOHN 1:4

You shall teach [God's laws] to your sons . . . so that your days and the days of your sons may be multiplied on the land.

DEUTERONOMY 11:19, 21

MOM TO MOM

For my husband and me, passing on our faith to our children is a huge priority. We believe it is so important to show commitment and consistency. It's more than taking our kids to church or saying a prayer at the end of the day. Moses said, "You shall teach [God's commandments] diligently to your sons and shall talk of them when you sit in your house and when you walk by the way and when you lie down and when you rise up. You shall bind them as a sign on your hand and they shall be as frontals on your forehead. You shall write them on the doorposts of your house and on your gates" (Deuteronomy 6:7–9). It's never too soon to begin this instruction. When our kids learn early on that Jesus is their most amazing, most powerful, and most loving Savior, it's a lesson that is likely to stay with them for the rest of their lives and into eternity.

ACTION STEPS

1. Some parents are reluctant to talk about their faith because they want their kids to make their own choice. The problem is that the world won't wait—messages in the media and elsewhere will rush in to fill the void in your vulnerable child's mind. Ask yourself who you'd prefer to influence your child's beliefs, you or someone you've never met?

2. Even if your kids have committed their lives to Jesus, their faith will be challenged as they get older. Read your Bible, as well as books such as Lee Strobel's *The Case for Christ*. Form

an intelligent faith so you can explain the what and why of your beliefs, and share this with your children.

Heavenly Father, thank You for the privilege of teaching our children about You. Give us wisdom so that nothing will come between our kids and an intimate relationship with You.

46

abuse and addiction

I was abused physically and sexually as a child. Now I'm a new mom, and I'm scared that I could someday abuse my children.

THE LORD'S SOLUTION

Be strong and let your heart take courage; yes, wait for the LORD.

PSALM 27:14

The eye of the LORD is on those who fear Him, on those who hope for His lovingkindness, to deliver their soul from death.

PSALM 33:18–19

MOM TO MOM

My heart breaks for anyone who has suffered from physical or sexual abuse, or who is struggling with addiction to alcohol, drugs, or pornography. I have tremendous admiration for women and men who are actively rejecting the destructive behaviors from their past. For the sake of your children, if this is historical behavior in your family, you need to be the one who breaks the cycle. If you are determined—and if you educate yourself on proven methods for success and trust in God to take care of the rest—you can do it. Dealing with pain takes time, so don't be hard on yourself. Remember that the power of the Lord is greater even than this obstacle. Give it to Him daily in prayer. Taking the courageous steps to face your past or addiction, deal with it, and move on is a great indicator that the cycle will end with you.

ACTION STEPS

1. If you or someone close to you is dealing with abuse or addiction, talk about it with someone you trust, perhaps a counselor, pastor, or doctor. Denial is a destroyer. Acknowledging the issue and seeking help are the first steps to recovery.

2. Read 1 Corinthians 10:13, and remember that the Lord will always "provide the way of escape" from temptation. Surrender completely to Him—every hour and every minute, if necessary—and you will find the power to conquer your worst nightmare.

Dear God, sometimes the evil in the world seems so overwhelming. Please protect my children, and me, from every threat. Keep our hearts pure and focused only on You.

47

cherish your husband

I have three children, and all are doing well. My husband and I, however, seem to have drifted apart since we had kids. How do we get the magic back?

THE LORD'S SOLUTION

An excellent wife, who can find? . . . She does [her husband] good and not evil all the days of her life.

PROVERBS 31:10, 12

This I command you, that you love one another.

JOHN 15:17

MOM TO MOM

Sometimes we moms get so focused on caring for our children that we neglect another important member of the family: Dad. The truth is that one of the greatest gifts you can give your kids is a picture of a healthy, loving marriage. It may require a renewed commitment. Start by letting your husband—and children—see how much you cherish him and your time together. For example, protect and celebrate special days such as anniversaries and birthdays. I remember being offered an amazing business opportunity that was scheduled for the same day Greg and I planned to celebrate our anniversary. The choice was easy: I turned down the project and enjoyed being with my husband. When you set aside other issues to spend time with your spouse, it sends a message that he is first in your life. That's great for your marriage. It is also a demonstration of love that your children will remember for a lifetime.

ACTION STEPS

1. What is the state of your marriage? No matter how strong, any relationship will benefit from extra attention. What can you do this week to show your husband how much you love and appreciate him? Make a plan and follow through.

2. When was your last date? Schedule a time for just the two of you. What wives and husbands with children often need most is simply more time to talk.

3. If your marriage is in a hard place, consider professional mentoring or counseling. Most churches offer something like this to help couples over the rough patches in life. Get your relationship back on track before small issues turn into big ones.

Dear Jesus, I do love my husband. Thank You for sending him into my life! Help me to show him my deep appreciation and to rekindle our relationship in ways that are pleasing to You.

48

resolving conflict

Our family seems to argue constantly. Our little disagreements often turn into shouting matches. What can we do differently?

THE LORD'S SOLUTION

Remind them . . . to malign no one, to be peaceable, gentle, showing every consideration for all.

TITUS 3:1–2

Honor all people, love the brotherhood, fear God.

1 PETER 2:17

MOM TO MOM

We all have unique personalities and viewpoints, so conflict—with your husband and amongst your children—is inevitable. The question is, how will you deal with it? Fighting with your spouse in front of the kids is never a good idea, so try to "disagree agreeably." If necessary, take your discussion into another room and close the door. Conflicts between kids should be handled according to their maturity. Timeouts work for many young children. Another great idea is to place your kids on a "peace rug." They must share that space until they talk through and resolve their disagreement. No matter what the issue and who is in conflict, try to resolve the matter quickly so it doesn't boil over into bitterness. And above all else, teach your children and model for them that everyone deserves courtesy and respect, whether you agree with them or not. We all have value in the eyes of the Lord.

ACTION STEPS

1. Do you know this passage: "Do not let the sun go down on your anger, and do not give the devil an opportunity" (Ephesians 4:26–27)? What opportunity is Paul talking about? Discuss it with your husband and (if they are old enough) your kids.

2. Just as shouting at each other won't solve a problem, neither will staying silent about an issue that bothers you. Are there any unresolved concerns in your marriage? Write

them down, then schedule a quiet time when you can discuss them with your husband with love and respect.

3. Many conflicts can be avoided if expectations are voiced clearly. Are you communicating your expectations to your family? If not, tell them up front what you want. It can make all the difference.

Heavenly Father, give us wisdom to settle our family disagreements quickly and completely. Enable us to demonstrate honor and love with every word we speak.

49

you are a brand

Last week, while waiting to pick up my kids after school, I snapped at another mom who made a comment I didn't like. I apologized the next day, but I still wonder what the other moms who heard me are thinking.

THE LORD'S SOLUTION

Make it your ambition to lead a quiet life, to mind your own business and to work with your hands, just as we told you, so that your daily life may win the respect of outsiders.

1 THESSALONIANS 4:11–12 (NIV)

He was zealous for the honor of his God.

NUMBERS 25:13

MOM TO MOM

At Kathy Ireland Worldwide, we take the quality of our brand very seriously. Our reputation and business success depend on it. You may not realize that you, too, are a brand. You may think, *That's crazy. I'm a person, not a brand!* Whether we like it or not, however, each encounter with someone creates a lasting impression, and those impressions make up our brand. The question is, what kind of brand are we? Are we kind, loyal, innovative, efficient? Do we get results? Do we show up for work or appointments ten minutes early or are we perpetually late? Are we negative? Do we have trouble getting along with others? Do we bring our "personal stuff" with us wherever we go? And, most important for those of us who are believers, are we honoring the Lord with the quality of our brand? Our actions and attitude can make the difference in inspiring others to pursue Jesus. If our brand needs an update, let's make that change today.

ACTION STEPS

1. To test your brand, ask people you trust—those who are willing to speak the truth—what impressions you make with others. If you don't like what you hear, let go of any feelings of rejection and decide how to move forward.

2. What do you think Paul means by "lead a quiet life" in the passage above? How does this win the respect of others? Share your thoughts with your family.

Lord, I want You to use me in a way that will lead others to You. Grant me opportunities to reflect Your love and make my brand count for You.

50

budget, budget, budget

I know it's a mistake, but I'm so busy that I don't keep a budget. I have to admit that sometimes I don't even balance my checkbook!

THE LORD'S SOLUTION

*Make your ear attentive to wisdom . . . then you will discern the fear of the L*ORD *and discover the knowledge of God.*

PROVERBS 2:2, 5

*"The silver is Mine and the gold is Mine," declares the L*ORD *of hosts.*

HAGGAI 2:8

MOM TO MOM

It is astonishing that so many people don't know exactly what they're spending, how much money they have, and what their financial goals are for the future. To handle your finances well, it is vital that you keep a budget and establish a financial plan. If you're married and your spouse is the one handling your money, it's equally important for you to know where you stand. Examine your budget carefully. Is your spending supporting or sabotaging your priorities and goals? Where do you expect to be financially in five, ten, and twenty years? There is more at stake here than your personal financial picture. Remember that "The earth is the LORD's, and all it contains, the world, and those who dwell in it" (Psalm 24:1). Your money is really God's money. Are you honoring Him with the way you manage His resources? The sooner you address these questions, the better off you and your finances will be.

ACTION STEPS

1. If you aren't keeping a budget, begin tracking your spending today. Find a program you like in a book at the library or on the internet, or simply record your expenses in a notebook or computer, and divide them into categories: savings, housing, child care, insurance, transportation, entertainment, clothing, etc.

2. Once you have a handle on where your money is going, establish a spending plan and stick to it! Discipline is the key

here—once you hit your limit for the month, it's time to stop.

3. Consider enlisting the help of a financial planner. If you can't afford a certified public accountant, consult a nonprofit credit-counseling service. Many Christian organizations provide these services at no cost.

Dear God, I am so sorry that I often fail to honor You in the way I manage money. Let this be a new beginning for the way I handle our family finances.

51

the power of place

The minute I walk in the door of my home, I feel oppressed. Something about the look of our house just feels wrong.

THE LORD'S SOLUTION

*I waited patiently for the L*ORD*. . . . He brought me up out of the pit of destruction, out of the miry clay, and He set my feet upon a rock making my footsteps firm.*

PSALM 40:1–2

There is a time for every event under heaven . . . a time to keep and a time to throw away.

ECCLESIASTES 3:1, 6

MOM TO MOM

Never underestimate the power of place to either lift your spirits or take a toll on your emotional well-being. I urge you to step back and consider how your home makes you feel. You may not even realize that the atmosphere of your living space makes you tense, anxious, and depressed when it should leave you relaxed, encouraged, and happy. Does your furniture make you feel hemmed in and out of balance? Do the colors on the walls seem stuck in the past? Are you overwhelmed by one of the most common culprits of all: clutter? Make a wish list of what you'd like to change in your home. Start with the small changes today, and save up for the big ones. Schedule a Saturday to "clutter bust." Even a few changes will begin allowing the joyful person God created you to be to bloom.

ACTION STEPS

1. If clutter is bringing you down, it's time to fight back. Take on one room at a time. As you come to each item, either put it to use, preserve the memory with a picture, place it in a scrapbook, or get rid of it. Learn to let go. As you do, you'll rediscover the inviting home you once knew and loved.

2. Aromatherapy is an easy way to turn your home into a retreat. Fill your living space with scented candles, herbal sachets, potpourri, diffusers, and bowls of dried flowers. Put a few drops of essential oils—concentrates of flowers, plants,

and woods—in your bathroom soap dispenser or on your furnace air filters for a therapeutic effect.

Lord, I thank You for the blessing of my home. Grant me wisdom to make it all it can be so my family and I can more easily reflect the joy that You give to each one of us.

52

quality and quantity

My husband and I both work, so we don't spend as much time with the kids as we'd like. We do, however, try to give them our full attention when we're there. Isn't that what's important?

THE LORD'S SOLUTION

Little children, let us not love with word or with tongue, but in deed and truth.

1 JOHN 3:18

If we walk in the Light as He Himself is in the Light, we have fellowship with one another.

1 JOHN 1:7

MOM TO MOM

It's true that the quality of your interaction with your children is extremely important. If your family time is limited by work or other activities, it's crucial that you spend it wisely. Face-to-face bonding with your children should be a daily priority. That means time when you're not distracted by household chores, phone calls, or work-related worry. This is your chance to focus on your kids and find out what's happening in their lives: ask about school, read together, laugh, wipe away tears, and enjoy each other's company. As important as quality time is with your kids, though, I believe that quantity is just as significant. We cannot expect our kids to open up and share with us on our timetable. Those moments occur during the "nothing" times when we're sitting on the floor doing a puzzle together or just hanging out. Special memories start with a commitment by Mom and Dad to simply be there with their kids.

ACTION STEPS

1. Make the most of your time with your kids by encouraging them to share their feelings. When they do open up, show that you take them, their moods, and their opinions seriously. You'll be creating an inviting and joyful atmosphere for the entire family.

2. Setting aside time for your kids is a challenge for any family, and doubly so if you are divorced. If this is your situation, your children need face-to-face time with both par-

ents (if possible) more than ever. Are you doing all you can to be present in your kids' lives? If not, see what you can re-schedule to create new opportunities for quantity *and* quality time with your children.

Heavenly Father, we so need the blessing of time together as a family. Help me to fully engage in the lives of my children so they will understand how much I love them.

acknowledgments

The Anchor to my soul, firm and secure . . . my Rock, my Light, my Lord and Savior and best friend, Jesus Christ . . . with Him all things are possible.

Mom and Dad . . . for your great, unlimited, unconditional love . . . always being there . . . your powerful prayers . . . for leading me to the Lord and teaching by example that all things, including faith, require work.

Barbara . . . so much more than a mother-in-law . . . Phil . . . forever in our hearts.

Aunt Dorothy . . . a pillar of strength.

My beautiful sisters, Mary and Cynthia . . . childhood adventures together, today you and your loving families inspire and delight.

Erik, Jason, Jon, and Stephen . . . family.

Erik . . . your quiet strength, your tremendous generosity, your brilliant and clever mind, your trust, your sense of adventure, your wisdom.

Jason . . . my mentor and so much more . . . for helping me find my voice . . . and an audience to listen! . . . for multiplying your gifts to bless others in powerful ways . . . your enormous heart, your clear, focused, and brilliant vision, your listening ears and open arms.

Jon . . . my bro, your fierce and secure protection, your jovial and loving heart, your amazing eye and extraordinary talent . . . genius.

Stephen . . . your inspiring strength, your deep thoughtfulness, your loyalty, integrity, and brilliant and passionate genius that shatters limits.

Steve, Dee, Georgia, Miles, Konrad, Rocco, Ruben, Chris, Tony, Claude, Andre, Nicholas, Mitch, Joel, Zulma, Bart, Monica, Charlie, Maria, Felipa, Nittaya and Millie . . . the best team in the world. Thank you to you, your spouses, your loved ones, and especially your children.

Brittany . . . beautiful and strong.

Camille, Baret, Jenny, Kim, Dawn, Michelene, Sue, Cheri, Wanda, Missi, Jule, Jeannine and your beautiful families . . . your prayers, friendship, love and always giving more than you get.

Bessie . . . my hero . . . thank you for leading, teaching, and saving lives . . . you're a great inspiration! . . . love to you and your beautiful family.

Wyatt, Jacob, Joseph, Daniel, Sophia, Elijah, Junior . . . Sal, Mark, Grant, Dyan, Dana, and Paul . . . you mean more to me than words can express . . . you are treasures.

Our Niemann family leaders, Fritz, Linda, Camilla, Bill, Greg, Leila, Joe, Melinda, Tom, Jeri, Mary, Ron, Matt, Betty, Jim, and Sue . . . you and your families are amazing!

To our entire family tree with branches in Canada, England, Norway, and of course the USA.

Our Hawaii Ohana . . . Justin, Marisol, your beautiful sons and family . . . Kainoa, Bobbie Lee, and your families.

Peter Mainstain, Donna Melby, Miriam Wizman . . . for support, protection, and love.

John and Marilyn Moretz . . . from the very beginning and forever . . . my love for you is too often unexpressed. That love is powerful and written on my heart.

Gavin Perdue and the team at Comerica Bank . . . for having faith in us when others did not.

Marilyn McCoo and Billy Davis, Jr. . . . for your gifts of love, friendship, and fellowship.

The Schuller family . . . for always giving warm welcomes and offering your hearts in friendship.

Anita and Roxy Pointer . . . brave, beautiful, and always so excited!

Tim Mendelson . . . with love and much appreciation.

The Estrada family . . . Erik and Nanette, great parents and great friends. Thank you for always giving so much to others . . . especially to us.

The Haskell family . . . Sam, Mary, Sam, and Mary Lane . . . your love, kindness, and leadership are off the charts. God bless you.

Joan van Ark and Jack Marshall for kindness and constant friendship.

Sim and Dr. Debra Farar . . . your friendship demonstrates the power of love, kindness, and brilliance. Thank you for loving and never judging.

To the Sedghi family . . . each of you is a precious jewel.

Effy and Leah for true friendship and wisdom . . . in turbulence and beyond.

Kathy, Tony, and your glorious children for giving love and becoming family.

Harold and Dotty . . . you're an inspiration to us all! Marion, thank you for loving my guys.

Our brand partners, manufacturers, and retailers . . . for investing and believing every day.

Elise and the team at AEFK . . . for loving and changing lives.

Jonathan Exley, Kendra Richards, and Jose Manuel Morales . . . your creative gifts and love are extraordinary!

John and Chrys Howard and the team at Howard Books . . . our visit at the United Nations was the beginning of this book. Thank you for allowing moms everywhere to experience these solutions. May the love of our Lord surround you always.

James Lund . . . Jim, thank you for endless hours of extraordinary support . . . your great gifts as a writer and a man of faith brought this book to life. You made it possible for this book to be a conversation with busy moms rather than an "academic" effort.

The Tarte and Fisher families . . . for lasting friendship and indescribable adventures.

The Kuchmas family . . . for caring, for inspiring, for your friendship.

The Dellar family . . . for being examples and being with us.

The Providence Hall board, Randy, Greg, Cliff, Andrew, Stretch, Elise, Kelly, David, Joy, Jay, Paulette, Laura, Brian . . . commitment, passion, wisdom, and perseverance.

The Davies, the Dusebouts, and the ELMO board . . . leading with character and wisdom.

Pastor Britt, Pastor G, and your families . . . your tremendous love of our Lord, your faithfulness, commitment, and desire to serve Him.

Bible-study ladies . . . your wisdom and encouragement.

The Merrick/Morgan home group and our entire church family . . . wisdom and accountability with love for each other and Him.

Even with this list, there are so many people who made this journey and book possible who are not mentioned here. Please know my gratitude and love for you is strong. Scripture speaks of thanking God for each remembrance . . . whether I've named you here or not, I give thanks for each and every one of you.

about the author

*K*athy Ireland is one of the top ten advocates for women's health in America, according to UCLA. Kathy is Fashion CEO of Kathy Ireland Worldwide (KIWW), the mission of which is "finding solutions for families, especially busy moms."™ KIWW and its brand partners design and produce more than fifteen thousand home and lifestyle products sold in over twenty-eight countries. Forbes reports KIWW sales at more than $1 billion annually. The Associated Press calls Kathy "a best friend to working mothers." Kathy says, "All moms work whether they get paid or not." Moms around the world embrace her designs, products, and solutions for living. The cornerstone of Kathy's life is her Christian faith. She is a mom, wife, and Sunday-school teacher. A former model, Kathy says, "I was okay but never super . . . my job description was to 'shut up and pose.' " Today Kathy is celebrated for her entrepreneurial gifts, philanthropy, and motivational speaking. Her voice is heard by audiences worldwide. She and her husband, Greg, have three children and live in Southern California. Kathy's best friend, Lord, and Savior is Jesus Christ.